Chesterton's Tavern

Praise for *Chesterton's Tavern*

The tavern plays an important role in the history of literature, theology and ideas. *Chesterton's Tavern*, as appropriately portrayed by historian Kevin Belmonte, is a homely place, comfortably situated for a refreshing and truly restorative introduction to the wisdom, wit, and remarkably relevant vision of Gilbert Keith Chesterton.

Belmonte's short but satisfyingly deep draft of vintage Chesterton can help us see that the essayist, critic, novelist, poet and popular theologian is for the ages. This book captures how Chesterton somehow carries no less than the wonder and secret of the universe in his farsighted yet down-to-earth paradoxes, parables and observations.

—Colin Duriez, author of *The Oxford Inklings*
and *Tolkien and Lewis: The Gift of Friendship*

Kevin Belmonte has given us, in this slim yet robust volume, a warm welcome to join a conversation *in medias res* at the Fleet Street Tavern with that master of conviviality, G.K. Chesterton.

With characteristic intellect, wit, and tender heart, GKC invites us to sit, raise a flagon, and join the conversation of the ages—resisting our addiction to the zeitgeist of "progress" and to learn from the wisdom of tradition. Yet Belmonte is not offering a notion of tradition as a thing preserved in amber, but a living spirit of love and truth and wonder.

With GKC acting as his spokesman, the writer offers us a genuine glimpse of this great man's vision—The Tavern at the End of the World— wherein all are friends, all raise a glass, all celebrate the greatest joy: the childlike love of God and the great surprise that Truth is a far more wondrous thing than even the wildest fictions can evoke.

—Bruce Herman, Lothlorien Distinguished Chair in Fine Arts, Gordon College

Chesterton's Tavern

A GREAT WRITER'S THOUGHTS ON LIFE AND THINGS OF WISDOM

KEVIN BELMONTE

Published by Canon Press
P.O. Box 8729, Moscow, ID 83843
800-488-2034 | www.canonpress.com

Kevin Belmonte, *Chesterton's Tavern: A Great Writer's Thoughts on Life and Things of Wisdom*

First published in 2016 by the author

Cover design by James Engerbretson
Interior layout by Valerie Anne Bost
Printed in the United States of America

Library of Congress Cataloging-in-Publication Data

Belmonte, Kevin Charles, author.
Chesterton's tavern : a great writer's thoughts on life and things of wisdom / Kevin Belmonte.
Moscow, Idaho : Canon Press, [2021]
LCCN 2021041013 | ISBN 9781954887206 (paperback)
LCSH: Chesterton, G. K. (Gilbert Keith), 1874-1936—Appreciation. | Chesterton, G. K. (Gilbert Keith), 1874-1936—Quotations. | Christianity—Quotations, maxims, etc. | Wisdom—Quotations, maxims, etc.
Classification: LCC PR4453.C4 Z533 2021 | DDC 828/.91209 [B]—dc23
LC record available at https://lccn.loc.gov/2021041013

22 23 24 25 26 27 28 29 30 10 9 8 7 6 5 4 3 2 1

To Malcolm Guite . . .

for memories of tavern time in Hamilton,

and the treasured gift of a 1935 copy of *G.K.'s Weekly*,

once part of Dorothy Sayers's library . . .

I cannot remember when I first met Chesterton. I was so much struck by a review of Scott's *Ivanhoe* which he wrote for the *Daily News* [in 1901]...that I wrote to him asking who he was and where he came from, as he was evidently a new star in literature.

—George Bernard Shaw

[Chesterton] is the only one I know who has the gift of Samuel Johnson.... One wants to hear what he has to say on any subject.

—Garry Wills

Chesterton's a classic.

—Ernest Hemingway

Contents

Preface

> Chesterton's times were much more like our own than we imagine.
>
> —William Oddie

The idea for this slender book owes more than a little to Alister McGrath's fine, discerning, and instructive text *If I Had Lunch with C.S. Lewis.*[1] The following pages tap the same conceit, save one difference . . .

This book imagines several "Fleet Street Tavern" meetings with Chesterton, circa 1912—a series of once-a-week dinners with him, holding forth in the evening, much as Samuel Johnson used to do at London's Mitre tavern.

Chesterton greatly admired Johnson, and sometimes appeared in Johnsonian costume—always with great relish. They were in many respects kindred spirits: richly enjoying fine tavern fare, trenchant conversation,

1. *If I Had Lunch with C.S. Lewis: Exploring the Ideas of C.S. Lewis on the Meaning of Life* (Carol Stream, IL: Tyndale, 2014).

and thoughtful reflection. Among the most revealing literary compliments Chesterton ever paid was one bestowed on Johnson, who, he said, could "walk into the heart without knocking."[2]

Chesterton, as a man of letters, was one of the early twentieth century's famous public intellectuals, and a journalist with a brilliant mind. The Irish playwright George Bernard Shaw was one contemporary to acknowledge his genius, while the American writer Ernest Hemingway once said, "Chesterton's a classic." Scholars too have noted his gifts, *The Oxford Reader's Companion to Charles Dickens* calling him "the greatest of all Dickens critics."[3] Poet T.S. Eliot said in 1927, "There is no better critic of Dickens living,"[4] while the philosopher William James said Chesterton's book *Charles Dickens: A Critical Study* was "as good as Rabelais."[5]

Chesterton's novel *The Man Who Was Thursday* was one of several classic works from his pen. Others, according to Pulitzer Prize writer Garry Wills, include "one brilliant biblical essay (on the Book of Job), one

2. Quoted in Maisie Ward, *Gilbert Keith Chesterton* (New York: Sheed & Ward, 1943), 232.

3. Quoted in Paul Schlicke, ed., *The Oxford Companion to Charles Dickens* (New York: Oxford University Press, 2011), 135.

4. T.S. Eliot, *Selected Essays 1917–1932* (New York: Harcourt Brace, 1932), 374.

5. Quoted in Ian Ker, *G.K. Chesterton: A Biography* (New York: Oxford University Press, 2011), 184.

superb piece of Shakespeare criticism (on *A Midsummer Night's Dream*), one neglected masterpiece in narrative verse (*The Ballad of the White Horse*), . . . one dark joke of a playlet (*The Surprise*), [and] one gripping short story ("The Flying Stars")."[6]

Chesterton's prose study of the painter G.F. Watts is, for Wills, yet another place where eloquence and insight shone—as in Chesterton's thoughts on the limits of words for expressing the soul: "There are in the soul tints more bewildering, more numberless, and more nameless than the colours of an autumn forest."[7]

Nor could Wills withhold just praise for Chesterton's gifts as a poet, as in his stirring translation of du Bellay's "Heureux qui comme Ulysse," which ends with:

> More than your Tiber is my Loire to me,
> Than Palatine, my little Lyré there;
> And more than all the winds of all the sea
> The quiet kindness of the Angevin air.[8]

6. Garry Wills, "A Chesterton for the Religious Right," *Christian Century* (May 1990): 532–33, in Religion Online, https://religion-online.org/article/a-chesterton-for-the-religious-right/.

7. Chesterton, "Watts' Allegorical Paintings," in *On Lying in Bed and Other Essays*, ed. Alberto Manguel (Calgary: Bayeux Arts, 2000), 156. For Willis's praise, see *Chesterton* (New York: Random House, 1961), 81.

8. Chesterton, "Translation from Du Bellay," *The Collected Works of G.K. Chesterton*, comp. Aidan Mackey, vol. 10, *Collected Poetry: Part 1* (San Francisco: Ignatius Press, 1994), 374.

And indeed, these are fine, revealing chapters of Chesterton's writing life. But more to the point of this book was his abiding influence on C.S. Lewis, as Dr. McGrath has described in his book. Things of faith were the heart of it all. "The great British apologist G.K. Chesterton," McGrath has said, "was much admired by Lewis." Reading Chesterton helped Lewis see that "faith provided a rich and realistic way of seeing, understanding, and experiencing the world."[9]

This was Chesterton's story.

What better then, remembering Chesterton's career as a journalist, than to imagine a set of weekly meetings that cordially "turn the tables" on him in the guise of interviews and discussion, exploring key tenets of his worldview?

So saying we may travel, as it were, to Edwardian London. There Chesterton, garbed in slouch hat, cape, and a sword-stick cane, waits at Fleet Street Tavern.

9. Alister McGrath, *If I Had Lunch with C.S. Lewis* (Carol Stream, IL: Tyndale, 2014), 13, 108.

CHAPTER ONE

At Once Old and New

The first of the intellectual beauties of the Book of Job is that it is all concerned with this desire to know the actuality; the desire to know what is, and not merely what seems.

—FROM CHESTERTON'S INTRODUCTION TO *THE BOOK OF JOB* (1907)

As we enter Fleet Street Tavern on the first evening, going to a backroom table flanked by high-back settles, we see Chesterton is already *in medias res,* in fine animated talk with a friend nearby about a favorite subject: Charles Dickens.

"But we have a long way to travel," Chesterton is heard to say, "before we get back to what Dickens *meant:* and the passage is along a rambling English road, a twisting road such as Mr. Pickwick travelled." Here he pauses for emphasis, then continues with a knowing look:

> But this at least is part of what [Dickens] meant; that comradeship and serious joy are not interludes in our travel; but that rather our travels are interludes in comradeship and joy, which through God shall endure forever. The inn does not point to the road; the road points to the inn. And all roads point at last to an ultimate inn, where we shall meet Dickens and all his characters: and when we drink again it shall be from the great flagons in the tavern at the end of the world.[1]

Then, with a quick rap of his sword-stick on the stout oak floor, Chesterton concludes, "And there, my good sir, you have it. What would be better!"

Then, with a turn, Chesterton sees we have arrived, and bids us welcome. "Pray, be seated," he might say, pointing to our table. And it's easy to see that he's been looking forward to this first visit.

Sitting down himself, Chesterton could well return to his love of London and its taverns—sharing thoughts to get the conversation started, like those from his book *All Things Considered:* "[Dickens] . . . said he could not think without the London streets. The London taverns heard always the quaintest conversation,

1. *Charles Dickens: A Critical Study* (New York: Dodd, Mead & Co., 1906), 300. Emphasis added.

whether it was Ben Jonson's at the Mermaid or Sam Johnson's at the Cock."[2]

After this, and once everyone's dinner orders have been taken, it's clear that Chesterton's only too ready to field questions, and so one of our company begins, round-robin fashion, by saying, "You've spoken at length about Christianity in your book *Orthodoxy.* For those who don't know your writings, what is Christianity, and what is orthodoxy?"

Here, Chesterton would say that in his book "the central Christian theology [is] summarized in the Apostles' Creed." And as for orthodoxy, it quite simply "means the Apostles' Creed."[3]

After this, a follow-up question is given: "What led you to write *Orthodoxy*?"

Smiling and laughing a little, Chesterton might admit, as indeed he did say in the introduction for *Orthodoxy,* that he was "a person only too ready to write books upon the feeblest provocation." A fine instance of his ready wit.

But in truth, he'd say, *Orthodoxy* was prompted by "several critics for whose intellect I have a warm respect (I may mention specially Mr. G.S. Street) [who] said that it was all very well for me to tell everybody

2. *All Things Considered* (New York: John Lane, 1909), 10. Originally published in the *Illustrated London News,* September 15, 1906.

3. *Orthodoxy* (New York: John Lane, 1909), 20.

to affirm his cosmic theory, but that I had carefully avoided supporting my precepts with example. 'I will begin to worry about my philosophy,' said Mr. Street, 'when Mr. Chesterton has given us his.'"[4]

And so, with *Orthodoxy,* Chesterton did—"giving an account," as he phrased it, "of my own growth in spiritual certainty."[5]

Here, having touched on the subject of philosophy, Chesterton has opened the discussion on a larger field. For a philosophy is something we all have, whether we realize it or not—an outlook on life that guides our words and actions.

They key, he would contend, is to discover a philosophy worthy of our trust, something that endures, and comports with the truth of things—a philosophy that justly tells us who we are, and who we are meant to be.

At the same time, he'd affirm that we mustn't allow ourselves to be taken in by fads, or be led astray by the idea that one's philosophy "moves with the times." Best understood, a true philosophy rests in things unchanging, like points on a map.

Regarding these things, Chesterton has much to tell us, for he treated them at length in his book. There, he said, a habit had "arisen in modern controversy of saying that such and such a creed can be held in one age but

4. *Orthodoxy*, 13.

5. *Orthodoxy*, 264.

cannot be held in another"—people who said that some teaching "was credible in the twelfth century, but is not credible in the twentieth." Chesterton begged to differ:

> You might as well say that a certain philosophy can be believed on Mondays, but cannot be believed on Tuesdays. You might as well say of a view of the cosmos that it was suitable to half-past three, but not suitable to half-past four. What a man can believe depends upon his philosophy, not upon the clock or the century.[6]

Few things could be more helpful than Chesterton's insights here, especially the last sentence. It is the *type* and *character* of a philosophy that is paramount, not whether it emerged yesterday, or the day after. Put another way, a philosophy that is worthy of the name ought to be *timeless*—true and salutary in any age.

But, Chesterton knew, there was still another consideration—and one of the highest import. This consideration was the *causa prima*, or prime cause, which led him to write the prequel to *Orthodoxy.* It was a book called *Heretics,* and while Chesterton was writing it, one thought was preeminent in his mind.

"In our time," Chesterton said, "philosophy or religion, our theory, that is, about ultimate things, has

6. *Orthodoxy*, 135–36.

been driven out, more or less simultaneously, from two fields which it used to occupy," literature and politics.[7] This was troubling, so Chesterton sought to defend the place of ultimate things.[8] Like a town crier of old, he spoke in the thoroughfares of his time, England 1905. "Persistently," he said,

> for the last twenty years the ideals of order or liberty have dwindled in our books; the ambitions of wit and eloquence have dwindled in our parliaments. Literature has purposely become less political; politics have purposely become less literary. General theories of the relation of things have thus been extruded from both; and we are in a position to ask, "*What have we gained or lost by this extrusion?* Is literature better, is politics better, for having discarded the moralist and the philosopher?"[9]

Chesterton was a writer of deep discernment. While many contemporaries, for example, saw Mark Twain solely as a colorful, endless fount of good humor, Chesterton saw the somberness that infused so much of his writing. As the noted biographer Ron Powers has said, "Twain

7. *Heretics* (London: John Lane, 1905), 16.
8. A point made cogently by Garry Wills in *Chesterton,* (New York: Doubleday, 2001), 108–109.
9. *Heretics*, 16–17. Emphasis added.

insisted that the secret source of humor was not joy, but sorrow. G. K. Chesterton was among [the few] who noticed this sometimes subtle dialectic . . . . Twain was 'always serious to the point of madness,' he observed—'an unfathomably solemn man.'"[10] So in taking the measure of his own historical moment, Chesterton could lay claim to wisdom.[11] As he watched and listened, he saw England beset by disquieting things. "Our affairs," he said,

> are hopelessly muddled by strong, silent men. And just as this repudiation of big words and big visions has brought forth a race of small men in politics, so it has brought forth a race of small men in the arts. Our modern politicians claim the colossal license of Caesar and the Superman, claim that they are too practical to be pure and too patriotic to be moral; but the upshot of it all is that a mediocrity is Chancellor of the Exchequer. Our new artistic philosophers call for the same moral license, for a freedom to wreck heaven and earth with their energy; but the upshot of it all is that a mediocrity is Poet Laureate.[12]

10. Ron Powers, *Mark Twain: A Life* (New York: Simon and Schuster, 2005), 89; see also 396.

11. Michael Ffinch, *G.K. Chesterton* (San Francisco: Harper, 1986), 161. "Critics were mostly agreed that [with *The Man Who Was Thursday*] Chesterton had produced an extraordinary fantasy, behind which . . . lurked 'a great, serious mission (for Mr. Chesterton, like all clowns, is intensely serious).'"

12. *Heretics*, 18–19.

Yet the trouble, for Chesterton, went deeper than baleful trends in public affairs. Many leaders of the literati—people with considerable influence in shaping public opinion—cared less and less about whether they were philosophically right. Words were ceasing to mean things they had formerly meant. First things were increasingly neglected; and this milieu had also corrupted the meaning of the words *heresy* and *orthodoxy.* Heresy, Chesterton wrote, "not only means no longer being wrong; it practically means being clear-headed and courageous." It had become commonplace for people to say, "I suppose I am very heretical," and seek applause. Meanwhile, the word *orthodoxy* had become a pariah. "It not only no longer means being right," Chesterton said, "it practically means being wrong."[13] And here, he sketched a scenario marked by rueful satire. "It is foolish," he wrote,

> generally speaking, for a philosopher to set fire to another philosopher in Smithfield Market because they do not agree in their theory of the universe. That was done very frequently in the last decadence of the Middle Ages, and it failed altogether in its object. But there is one thing that is infinitely more absurd and unpractical than burning a man for his philosophy . . . the habit of saying that his philosophy does

13. *Heretics*, 12.

> not matter . . . . Mr. Bernard Shaw has put the view in a perfect epigram: "The golden rule is that there is no golden rule." We are more and more to discuss details in art, politics, literature. A man's opinion on tramcars matters; his opinion on Botticelli matters; his opinion on all things does not matter. He may turn over and explore a million objects, but he must not find that strange object, the universe; for if he does he will have a religion, and be lost.[14]

Chesterton was grieved that many contemporaries now disdained the moral and intellectual heritage handed down to them. To further explain what he meant, he described things still with us, one hundred years on:

> When the old Liberals removed the gags from all the heresies, their idea was that religious and philosophical discoveries might thus be made. Their view was that cosmic truth was so important that every one ought to bear independent testimony. The modern idea is that cosmic truth is so unimportant that it cannot matter what any one says. The former freed inquiry as men loose a noble hound; the latter frees inquiry as men fling back into the sea a fish unfit

14. *Heretics*, 12–13. Garry Wills has written with great perception on Chesterton's taking the intellectual "measure" of Shaw. See *Chesterton*, 143–45.

> for eating. Never has there been so little discussion about the nature of men as now, when, for the first time, any one can discuss it. The old restriction meant that only the orthodox were allowed to discuss religion. Modern liberty means that nobody is allowed to discuss it.[15]

Given this, Chesterton cast his reasons for writing *Heretics* in one sentence: "But there are some people, nevertheless—and I am one of them—who think that the most practical and important thing about a man is still his view of the universe."[16] So he surveyed the cultural landscape—to unriddle and refute prevalent heresies. It was never too late to regain lost ground. He could foster that good end.

To explain his purpose, and set the stage for his book, Chesterton employed an ancient literary device: the parable. He asked his readers to

> suppose that a great commotion arises in the street about something, let us say a lamp-post, which many influential persons desire to pull down. A grey-clad monk, who is the spirit of the Middle Ages, is approached upon the matter, and begins to say, in the arid manner of the Schoolmen, "Let us first of all

15. *Heretics*, 14–15.

16. *Heretics*, 15.

> consider, my brethren, the value of Light. If Light be in itself good—"
>
> At this point, he is somewhat excusably knocked down. All the people make a rush for the lamp-post, the lamp-post is down in ten minutes, and they go about congratulating each other on their unmediaeval practicality. But as things go on they do not work out so easily. Some people have pulled the lamp-post down because they wanted the electric light; some because they wanted old iron; some because they wanted darkness, because their deeds were evil. Some thought it not enough of a lamppost, some too much; some acted because they wanted to smash municipal machinery; some because they wanted to smash something. *And there is war in the night, no man knowing whom he strikes.* So, gradually and inevitably, to-day, to-morrow, or the next day, there comes back the conviction that the monk was right after all, and that all depends on what is the philosophy of Light. Only what we might have discussed under the gas-lamp, we now must discuss in the dark.[17]

Chesterton's parable wasn't one of despair, but a plea to say sound thinking about philosophy could avert the trouble it painted. And if "philosophy or religion, our theory, that is, about ultimate things" had been driven

17. *Heretics*, 23–24. Emphasis added.

out "from two fields which it used to occupy,"[18] literature and politics, it could be driven back in—or welcomed once more to its rightful place. That was worth his best efforts.

18. *Heretics*, 16.

CHAPTER TWO

Mere Chronology

To have known the things that from the weak are furled,
Perilous ancient passions, strange and high;
It is something to be wiser than the world,
It is something to be older than the sky.

—FROM "THE GREAT MINIMUM" (1915)

From the start of our second dinner gathering at Fleet Street Tavern, it seems clear that Chesterton wishes to pick up right where he left off at the close of the first evening. Since that gathering was largely devoted to a plea for sound philosophical thinking, or the place reflections about ultimate things should have in our lives, he would say we also need to guard against the siren song of "mere chronology."

What is "mere chronology," we might ask?

Chesterton could tell us that in a column for the *Illustrated London News,* he had written, "I find some old thoughts that are also true, but which are so old that many modern people had dropped them, *merely because they were old.*"[1]

That is, people were spurning ideas on the basis of mere chronology alone. Or, to put it another way, there was a growing disdain for any notion of timeless truth and wisdom—something much to be regretted.

And yet, Chesterton would say, there is more to consider: an ever-growing fascination with what could be called "new thought." Once more, he could tell us, he'd written about this in the *Illustrated London News,* addressing it directly with a cogent question, couched in Mark Twain–like wit:

> What is the New Thought? And who thought it? This is a very mysterious matter which has exhausted all my slender talents as an amateur detective. I know I am laying no light burden on myself and my local postman in asking such a question, for the people in movements such as this always assume that you know nothing about the movement, and proceed to tell you all about it on reams and reams of letter-paper. But this is not my difficulty. My difficulty is that I have read what is to be said about the New Thought; I have read columns and columns about it;

1. "What Is the New Thought?," in *Collected Works*, vol. 29, *The Illustrated London News: 1911–1913*, ed. Lawrence J. Clipper (San Francisco: Ignatius Press, 1915), 458.

> it is the thought that I cannot find. A new thought is a very rare thing, and it would be a magnificent creature to catch. The only things I can think of that one would really call "new thoughts" would be certain celebrated jokes, certain scientific discoveries, and a few less frequent cases of a really original argument used in an old controversy.[2]

Here, Chesterton might tell us he published this column under a masthead banner showing a court jester, taking notes amid a company of pilgrims looking for all the world as though they stepped from the pages of Chaucer's *Canterbury Tales.* It's a fitting image, he might say, as we should ever be on the lookout for revealing stories of the human condition. And beneath the jester's guise he'd adopted was a trove of good truths, chief of which is that much or virtually all of what we might consider "new thought" is really "old thought," or ideas and beliefs that have been around a very long time.

If we miss this, we are twice impoverished.

For Chesterton had written of something else on the near horizon: the threat posed by "the cult of the future."[3] Here we might see his words apply, with

2. "What Is the New Thought?," 457.

3. This and the remaining quotes in this chapter are from Chesterton, *What's Wrong with the World?* (London: Cassell, 1910), 37. Emphasis added.

no less truth, to our time. And it's all something, he might add, he'd written of in his book *What's Wrong with the World*—published in 1910. "The last few decades," he'd said,

> have been marked by a special cultivation of the romance of the future. We seem to have made up our minds to misunderstand what *has* happened; and we turn, with a sort of relief, to stating what *will* happen—which is (apparently) much easier.[4]

The more he'd thought about this, Chesterton came to feel the modern mind was being ineluctably "propelled towards the coming time." It had been, in the words of a popular phrase, "knocked into the middle of next week."[5]

But why? What goad drove the modern mind so relentlessly?

Chesterton reasoned it couldn't be "an affection for futurity" as a *known* quantity. "Futurity," he said, "does not exist, because it is *still* future." No, he was quite certain it was something else, and for him, that something was "a fear of the past; a fear not merely of the evil in the past, but of the good in the past also."

4. *What's Wrong with the World?*, 36.

5. Remaining quotes from this page are from *What's Wrong with the World?*, 27. Emphasis added.

This fear was aided and abetted by "the romance of the future" he described earlier. Its allure lay in the perception that the future is infinitely malleable—to be fashioned into any desired shape. The future is something of our design—a place where we, as monarchs of hypothetical realms, can ostensibly banish all hardship, and find only good things. Futurity promises broad, sunlit uplands. It promises utopia. Simply have done with the past, and all surely will be well.

Chesterton put it this way:

> The future is a blank wall on which every man can write his own name as large as he likes; the past I find already covered with illegible scribbles, such as Plato, Isaiah, Shakespeare, Michael Angelo . . . . I can *make* the future as narrow as myself; the past is *obliged* to be as broad and turbulent as humanity. And the upshot of this modern attitude is really this: that men invent new ideals because they dare not attempt old ideals. They look forward with enthusiasm, because they are afraid to look back.[6]

Yet there was, unavoidably, "a narrowness" in this cavalcade of new ideas: its "limiting effect of the future." Modern prophetic idealism was narrow, Chesterton said, "because it has undergone a persistent process of

6. *What's Wrong with the World?*, 27–28.

elimination. We must ask for new things because we are not *allowed* to ask for old things."[7]

This was a mindset no less flawed than it was misguided.

As Chesterton wrote, "[It] is based on this idea that we have got all the good that can be got out of the ideas of the past." However, he said, "we have *not* got all the good out of them." And perhaps, at the present time, "not *any* of the good out of them."

There was a great need for something more. Chesterton called it by name: the need of a "complete freedom for *restoration* as well as revolution."

The more he thought about it, the more he detected a churlish belligerence in all this talk of "new ideas." Here, he said,

> We often read nowadays of the valour or audacity with which some rebel attacks a hoary tyranny, or an antiquated superstition. There is not really any courage at all in attacking hoary or antiquated things, any more than in offering to fight one's grandmother. The really courageous man is he who defies tyrannies young as the morning, and superstitions fresh as the first flowers.[8]

7. Remaining quotes from this page are from *What's Wrong with the World?*, 32. Emphasis added

8. *What's Wrong with the World?*, 32–33.

This led Chesterton to contemplate the nature of free thought, and what intellectual courage really looked like. It brought a polar star to chart his course.

"The only true free-thinker," he said, "is he whose intellect is as much free from the future as from the past. He cares as little for what will be as for what has been; he cares only for what *ought* to be."[9]

Warming to this theme, he said, "For my present purpose, I specially insist on this abstract independence. If I am to discuss what is wrong, one of the first things that are wrong is this: the deep and silent modern assumption that past things have become impossible."[10]

Chesterton stoutly rejected this assumption, and then set a sacred metaphor of modernity clearly in his sights.

"There is," he wrote, "one metaphor of which the moderns are very fond; they are always saying, '*You can't put the clock back*.'" That, Chesterton believed ardently, was anything but true. He said the simple and obvious answer was: "*You can.*"

Here, he cast a trenchant metaphor of his own.

A clock, he said, is "a piece of human construction." It can be restored by its makers "to any figure or hour."

9. *What's Wrong with the World?*, 33. Emphasis added.

10. Remaining quotes from this page are from *What's Wrong with the World?*, 33. Emphasis added.

This image held another still more salutary application.

"In the same way," Chesterton observed, "society, being a piece of human construction, can be reconstructed upon any plan that has ever existed."

Having set this clock, Chesterton gave a ringing declaration of moral liberty. "This is, as I say, the first freedom that I claim: *the freedom to restore.*"

Yet here, he'd only just begun to write. "Now in history," he said,

> there is no Revolution that is not a Restoration. Among the many things that leave me doubtful about the modern habit of fixing eyes on the future, none is stronger than this: that all the men in history who have really done anything with the future have had their eyes fixed upon the past. I need not mention the Renaissance, the very word proves my case. The originality of Michael Angelo and Shakespeare began with the digging up of old vases and manuscripts.[11]

Chesterton closed with a suasive plea for his contemporaries not to reject so many good things from their common inheritance—things still good for use—tools that could shape the good society.

11. *What's Wrong with the World?*, 28.

And if groupthink was bent on rejecting them, he steadfastly refused to.

"I merely declare my independence," he said, "*I merely claim my choice of all the tools in the universe . . . .* I shall not admit that any of them are blunted merely because they have been used."[12]

12. *What's Wrong with the World?*, 35; emphasis added.

CHAPTER THREE

What Does Progress Look Like?

Somebody wants a Wiser Age, . . .
And grey with dust is Dante's crest,
The bell of Rabelais soundless swings;
And the winds come out of the west.

—FROM "A BALLADE OF A BOOK-REVIEWER" 1908)

At our third Fleet Street Tavern gathering, it would not be surprising for Chesterton to voice some as-yet-unspoken concerns about "the cult of the future." One word was ever present in current discourse: *progress*—all the more troubling as such talks seemed untethered to any kind of agreement on first principles.

Chesterton described this scenario by saying,

The case of the general talk of "progress" is, indeed, an extreme one. As enunciated to-day, "progress" is

> simply a comparative of which we have not settled the superlative. We meet every ideal of religion, patriotism, beauty, or brute pleasure with the alternative ideal of progress—that is to say, we meet every proposal of getting something that we know about, with an alternative proposal of getting a great deal more of nobody knows what.[1]

Clearly, Chesterton saw that definitions matter.

Further, it's important to describe progress in ways worthy of our allegiance. Properly defined, progress has "a most dignified and legitimate meaning."[2] By its very name, he said, progress "indicates a direction."[3]

However, "used in opposition to precise moral ideals," the word *progress* is ludicrous. "Nobody," he said, "has any business to use the word 'progress' unless he has a definite creed."[4]

Here was the gist of it all. "I do not . . . say," Chesterton wrote,

> that the word "progress" is unmeaning; I say it is unmeaning without the previous definition of a moral doctrine, and that it can only be applied to groups

1. *Heretics*, 35.
2. *Heretics*, 35.
3. *Heretics*, 36.
4. *Heretics*, 35–36.

> of persons who hold that doctrine in common. Progress is not an illegitimate word, but it is . . . a sacred word, a word which could only rightly be used . . . in the ages of faith.[5]

Each of these cautionary thoughts about progress, Chesterton would say, are essential. They provide much needed clarity, highlighting ways in which progress, or our *perceptions* of it, can be misdirected. For tetherless perceptions of progress were a great dilemma of his time. "Here," as he stated,

> comes in the whole collapse and huge blunder of our age. We have mixed up two different things, two opposite things. Progress *should* mean that we are always changing the world to suit the vision. Progress does mean (just now) that we are always changing the vision.[6]

To change course, Chesterton would argue for a robust understanding of the word *reform*. Everything, he would insist here, rests on a guiding moral vision, shaped by "precise moral ideals."[7] Then, too, the word *reform* is also a metaphor signifying a "reasonable and

5. *Heretics*, 37.
6. *Orthodoxy*, 195.
7. *Heretics*, 35.

determined" people. "It means," said Chesterton, "that we see a certain thing out of shape, and we mean to put it into shape. And we know *what* shape."

Chesterton then gave a sterling phrase: "Reform implies *form*." That is to say, consensus and consistency were crucial. They could not be present if those calling for progress were "always changing the vision," to use his phrase.[8]

Progress, he declared, should rightly mean "we are slow but sure in bringing justice and mercy among men." But in a time of ever-changing vision, like his, true progress was wounded by doubt over what things like justice and mercy meant.

This was a source of genuine grief. For progress, as he said,

> *should* mean that we are always walking towards the New Jerusalem, [not] that the New Jerusalem is always walking away from us. We are not altering the real to suit the ideal. We are altering the ideal: it is easier.[9]

Next, Chesterton cast a parable, clothed in satire. It was like a splash of cold water for clarity's sake. "Let us suppose," he said,

8. Remaining quotes from this page are from *Orthodoxy*, 194–95. Emphasis added.

9. *Orthodoxy*, 195.

> [Suppose] a man wanted a particular kind of world; say, a blue world . . . . He could work away (in every sense) until all was blue. He could have heroic adventures; the putting of the last touches to a blue tiger, [or mythic] dreams; the dawn of a blue moon. But if he worked harm, that high-minded reformer would certainly (from his own point of view) leave the world better and bluer than he found it. If he altered a blade of grass to his favourite colour every day, he would get on slowly. But if he altered his favourite colour every day, he would not get on at all. If, after reading a fresh philosopher, he started to paint everything red or yellow, his work would be thrown away: there would be nothing to show except a few blue tigers walking about, specimens of his early bad manner. This is exactly the position of the average modern thinker.[10]

In his youth, Chesterton had trained at the Slade School of Fine Art in London. Standing before a canvas, palette in hand, he knew what it meant to "progress" with work on a new painting.

That time, and this imagery, now rallied to his aid as he sought to convey a vision of progress in society:

> This, therefore, is our first requirement about the ideal towards which progress is directed; *it must be fixed.*

10. *Orthodoxy*, 195–96.

> [James] Whistler used to make many rapid studies of a sitter; it did not matter if he tore up twenty portraits. But it would matter if he looked up twenty times, and each time saw a new person sitting placidly for his portrait. So it does not matter (comparatively speaking) how often humanity fails to imitate its ideal; for then all its old failures are fruitful. But it does frightfully matter how often humanity changes its ideal; for then all its old failures are fruitless.[11]

These images, and inferences, were lodestars of wisdom. In time, Chesterton hoped they would become shards of light for his fellow Britons. Tenets of wisdom from the past had their uses, after all. And they might be worth a second look.

One thing remained. Like a herald from ages past, Chesterton thought to unfurl a banner. He set it in place, and it flew as a royal standard from a high tower. It bore these thought-provoking words:

> Orthodoxy . . . is the natural fountain of revolution and reform.[12]

11. *Orthodoxy*, 199. Emphasis added.
12. *Orthodoxy*, 257.

CHAPTER FOUR

To Find the Eternal

A word came forth in Galilee, a word like to a star;
It climbed and rang and blessed and burnt wherever
brave hearts are.

—FROM "A WORD" (C. 1910)

To start our fourth Fleet Street Tavern gathering, a question might well arise as to just what Chesterton meant when he said, "Orthodoxy . . . is the natural fountain of revolution and reform."[1]

Here, he'd marshaled his well-known gift for paradox; but smiling at this, he would welcome the chance to explain his phrase.

Eternal verities, he would say, are the essence of orthodoxy. And when he discovered this, he wrote that the dogmas of Christianity "are far more fantastic, and, perhaps, far more beautiful than we think."[2]

1. *Orthodoxy*, 257.
2. *Heretics*, 303–304.

During his years as an art student, Chesterton had nearly been overwhelmed by scepticism and despair. Thinking himself "a lost soul," he barely "hung on to the remains of religion."[3] At last, he thought to re-examine Christianity. It proved a journey to "a convincing creed," written with "wonder and an idea of welcome."[4]

All within a faith two thousand years old.

"One searches for truth," he remembered, "but it may be that one pursues instinctively the more extraordinary truths."[5] That was his story.

Christianity was an ancient faith, yet a timeless faith—defying those who held only to "the cult of the future."[6] Saying yes to Christianity, Chesterton had become countercultural in their eyes. They weren't free to seek "the good in the past."[7]

He was.

And here he saw the tag "countercultural" as a badge of honor, saying, "He is only a very shallow critic who cannot see an eternal rebel in the heart of a Conservative."[8]

Today, the word *dogma* has a pejorative taint. To say someone is dogmatic is to describe a person unreasoningly steadfast in holding an opinion. The word

3. *Autobiography* (New York: Sheed & Ward, 1936), 94.

4. *Orthodoxy*, viii, 16.

5. *Orthodoxy*, 18.

6. "What Is the New Thought?," 457.

7. *What's Wrong with the World?*, 27.

8. *Varied Types* (New York: Dodd, Mead and Co., 1903), 252.

dogmatic refers to someone considered unyielding, and never in a positive way.

Such perceptions held true in Chesterton's time; and he thought it high time someone tried to rehabilitate the word. He knew the word *dogma* had a fine lineage—as meaning, quite simply, a "principle" or "tenet."[9] He also discerned another equally noble aspect of the word. A dogmatist, he maintained, "is interested only in the truth, and only in the truth because it is true."[10]

Chesterton also understood that dogmas lie at the very heart of who we are. "Man," he said,

> can be defined as an animal that makes dogmas. As he piles doctrine on doctrine and conclusion on conclusion in the formation of some tremendous scheme of philosophy and religion, he is, in the only legitimate sense of which the expression is capable, *becoming more and more human*. When he drops one doctrine after another in a refined scepticism, when he declines to tie himself to a system, when he says that he has outgrown definitions, when he says that he disbelieves in finality, when, in his own imagination, he sits as God, holding no form of creed but contemplating all, then he is by that very process sinking slowly

9. *The Concise Oxford Dictionary of Current English* (Oxford: Clarendon Press, 1912), 244.

10. "John Ruskin," in *The Book Fair* (London: Routledge & Sons, 1907), 6.

> backwards into the vagueness of the vagrant animals, and the unconsciousness of the grass. Trees have no dogmas. Turnips are singularly broad-minded.
>
> If then, I repeat, there is to be mental advance, it must be mental advance in the construction of a definite philosophy of life. And that philosophy of life must be right, and the other philosophies wrong.[11]

Chesterton's keen thoughts here about the myth of "refined scepticism" are deeply important. He rightly knew it wasn't as though there are only *some* people who make dogmas, while *others* live (more nobly) in dogma-free objectivity.

There are no such people.

Everyone holds dogmas, or certain ways of looking at the world. Some simply refuse to be honest about it, or the preference for *their* dogmas, as opposed to the dogmas of others. Chesterton captured this dynamic satirically: "The modern world is filled with men who hold dogmas so strongly that they do not even know that they are dogmas."[12]

And he robustly challenged those who thought themselves refined sceptics, with lives blissfully free of dogma.

It was all rhetorical hogwash, and he would have none of it.

11. *Heretics*, 286–87. Emphasis added.

12. *Heretics*, 302.

> There are two kinds of people in the world, the *conscious* dogmatists and the *unconscious* dogmatists. [And] I have always found myself that the unconscious dogmatists were by far the most dogmatic.[13]

* * *

Chesterton also rejected something no less troubling: the phenomenon of revolving-door dogmas, or tenets du jour. All about him, as noted above, there was an ever-growing chorus saying, "Such and such a creed can be held in one age but cannot be held in another." Delusive sophistry taxed his patience; and here, he did not hesitate to say no.

For if a dogma rightly reflected truth, it was timeless, not time bound—with some sort of expiration date. Allegiance to a dogma should flow from its fidelity to truth and have nothing to do with looking at one's watch.

Moreover, dogmas involve the making of value judgments. Some dogmas are deserving; others less so. But we must all make choices.

Chesterton accepted the truth claims of Christianity, one of a great company of souls to do so down the centuries.

13. *Generally Speaking* (London: Methuen, 1928), 20. This is a rephrasing of a sentence Chesterton published in the June 23, 1922 issue of the *New Witness*, 394: "In truth there are only two kinds of people; those who accept dogmas and know it, and those who accept dogmas and don't know it."

His hope for the future was rooted in an ancient faith. For him, things of the past brought immeasurable blessing. And sages from elder years helped him find lasting treasures about life and faith. He was deeply grateful for them.

Who they were, and what they said, will be taken up in chapters to follow.

CHAPTER FIVE

The Sage of Relics and Rumours

Or sane and sweet and sudden as a bird sings in the rain—
Truth out of Tusitala spoke and pleasure out of pain.
Yea, cool and clear and sudden as a bird sings in the grey,
Dunedin to Samoa spoke, and darkness unto day.

—FROM "TO EDMUND CLERIHEW BENTLEY" (1907)

In a column Chesterton wrote for the *Illustrated London News*, dated October 1908, he cast something of an unlikely writer in the role of a sage: Daniel Defoe, the author of *Robinson Crusoe.* At the outset of our fifth gathering at Fleet Street Tavern, he could tell us about this.

But first, a bit of background about Defoe and his famous book.

Published in 1719, *Robinson Crusoe* is one of the world's great adventure tales. Chesterton wrote about the book, and its author, many times. *Robinson Crusoe,* he believed, was a book with timeless wisdom for some of the great questions and concerns in life. His essay in the *Illustrated London News* explained this.

Many thought Defoe's book a vivid adventure of the sea, and faraway lands. Chesterton understood this, and richly enjoyed the book on that level. Yet at the same time, he looked to something more: *Robinson Crusoe* was great literature, and he could count the reasons.

First, Chesterton parted from those who considered Defoe's book *solely* an adventure tale. Its larger themes gave it a place of far greater import.

Defoe's narrative, he wrote,

> is not a story of adventure; rather it is a story of the absence of adventure—that is, in the first and best part of it. Twice Crusoe runs away to sea in disobedience, and twice escapes with wreck or other peril; the third time we feel that he is set apart for some strange judgment by God. [That] is the great central and poetical idea of *Robinson Crusoe.* It is a visitation not of danger, but of a dreadful security.[1]

A "poetical idea" in *Robinson Crusoe*? Surely not.

1. From *Collected Works*, ed. Lawrence J. Clipper, vol. 28, *The Illustrated London News, 1908–1910* (San Francisco: Ignatius Press, 1987), 203. Originally published in the *Illustrated London News,* October 24, 1908.

Yet Chesterton was in earnest. Daniel Defoe had deftly spun a theme of purpose and subtlety in his novel. As Chesterton explained,

> The salvage of Crusoe's goods, the comparative comfort of his life, the natural riches of his island, his human relations with many of the animals—all this is an exquisitely artistic setting for the awful idea of a man whom God has cast out from among men. A mere scurry of adventures would have left Crusoe no time for thinking; and the whole object of the book is to make Crusoe think.[2]

Reading *Robinson Crusoe* helped Chesterton consider life-altering questions, and he wrote more about them. As he described it, Defoe's classic text

> owes its eternal vivacity to the fact that it celebrates the poetry of limits, nay, even the wild romance of prudence. Crusoe is a man on a small rock with a few comforts just snatched from the sea: the best thing in the book is simply the list of things saved from the wreck. The greatest of poems is an inventory. Every kitchen tool becomes ideal because Crusoe might have dropped it in the sea. It is a good exercise, in empty or ugly hours of the day, to look at anything,

2. Ibid.

> the coal-scuttle or the book-case, and think how happy one could be to have brought it out of the sinking ship on to the solitary island. But it is a better exercise still to remember how *all things have had this hair's-breadth escape:* everything has been saved from a wreck. Every man has had one horrible adventure: as a hidden untimely birth he had not been, as infants that never see the light. Men spoke much in my boyhood of restricted or ruined men of genius: and it was common to say that many a man was a Great Might-Have-Been. To me it is a more solid and startling fact that any man in the street is a Great Might-Not-Have-Been.[3]

Robinson Crusoe was, in this light, a high and unexpected parable: centered on the gift of existence. But cast there, too, were impressions on "the poetry of limits," which countered the all-too-frequent tendency to take existence for granted. Defoe had discovered an ingenious, durable, and vivid way to remind everyone who read his book that their lives, for any number of reasons, *might not have been.*

Seen this way, life is a true, invaluable gift; one to prompt what Chesterton called a "mystical minimum of gratitude."[4] For Defoe's "adventure story" to achieve all this was rather extraordinary, when one stopped to

3. *Orthodoxy,* 115–16. Emphasis added.

4. *Autobiography,* 94.

think about it. Chesterton heralded this surmise with every fiber of his being, for as he'd said elsewhere,

> There is at the back of our lives an abyss of light, more blinding and unfathomable than any abyss of darkness; and it is the abyss of actuality, of existence, of the fact that things truly are, and that we are ourselves incredibly and sometimes almost incredulously real.[5]

And what of the very nature of good itself?

Here, too, Defoe had something deeply important to say. When, in his time of scepticism and despair, Chesterton sought some beacon of hope, he remembered his reading of *Robinson Crusoe.*

As he recalled in the pages of his own book *Orthodoxy*,

> There had come into my mind a vague and vast impression that in some way all good was a remnant to be stored, and held sacred out of some primordial ruin. Man had saved his good as Crusoe saved his goods: he had saved them from a wreck. All this I felt and the age gave me no encouragement to feel it. And all this time I had not even thought of Christian theology.[6]

5. *Chaucer* (New York: Farrar & Rinehart, 1932), 28.
6. *Orthodoxy*, 118.

For all these reasons, *Robinson Crusoe* gave light and wisdom. Chesterton thought to repay his debt to Daniel Defoe, and when he did, he penned one of the most telling prose passages found anywhere in his writings. "Good," he said,

> was not merely a tool to be used, but a relic to be guarded, like the goods from Crusoe's ship—even that had been *the wild whisper of something originally wise,* for, according to Christianity, we were indeed the survivors of a wreck, the crew of a golden ship that had gone down before the beginning of the world.[7]

To be sure, Chesterton saw *Robinson Crusoe* as a great work of art. But it was also a way station for his soul. As he paused there, he heard something on the wind: "the wild whisper of something originally wise."

He listened: finding faith, and the haven that will always remain.

7. *Orthodoxy,* 146. Emphasis added.

CHAPTER SIX

The Sage of a Thousand Stories

Here dies another day
During which I have had eyes, ears, hands
And the great world round me;
And with tomorrow begins another.
Why am I allowed two?

—FROM CHESTERTON'S EARLY NOTEBOOKS (C. 1894)

Much of his life, Chesterton felt an ardent debt to Robert Louis Stevenson. And having spoken, as it were, about Daniel Defoe and *Robinson Crusoe* in our sixth Fleet Street Tavern gathering, he would likely wish to speak next of Stevenson.

As for literary expressions of his debt, Chesterton could tell us that in 1901, he wrote an early and important essay called "The Mistake about Stevenson."[1] This

1. Chesterton's unsigned review, "The Mistake about Stevenson," appeared in the March 14, 1901, issue of the *Daily News*.

was followed still later by a book-length study of Stevenson's writing and ideas.

For during the time he wrestled with depression and despair, as stated in his autobiography, he'd begun reading a small cadre of fashionable writers, Stevenson among them, "who were not pessimists." Here Chesterton was especially grateful for Stevenson's stated "belief in the ultimate decency of things."[2]

True, such a phrase doesn't sound very subversive; but to reject pessimism so prominently at this time really was countercultural. Then, too, Stevenson had put the matter much more forcefully than Chesterton's brief quoting suggests.

"The poor things of a day look ruefully on," Stevenson had said of a trying time. Subject to bouts of debilitating ill health, he often struggled with depression.

Still, as he told his friend Sidney Colvin: "Does it shake my cast-iron faith? I cannot say it does. I believe in an ultimate decency of things; ay, and if I woke in hell, should still believe it!"[3]

Why was this so important to Chesterton?

The 1890s, as he came of age, were the years of the *fin de siècle* era. As scholar G.P. Landow has written, assumptions underlying much of the poetry, fiction

2. *Autobiography*, 94.

3. *The Works of Robert Louis Stevenson: Correspondence*, (Edinburgh: Constable, 1897), 283.

and art of this time centered on "an (anti-Romantic belief) . . . in fallen man and nature; [the] omnipresence of evil and the grotesque"; as well as a "lack of health, balance, and innocence." The mood of this period was a pervasive atmosphere of "ennui, incompleteness," displaying a deep "sense of loss, exile, isolation."[4]

Lines of verse Chesterton dedicated to his friend Edmund Bentley evoke this troubled time, and how it affected him as a young person:

> A cloud was on the minds of men, and wailing went the
> weather,
> Yea, a sick cloud upon the soul when we were boys
> together.[5]

Later in the poem, he spoke of "doubts that drove us through the night."[6] Chesterton was a sensitive young man, struggling to make sense of the world, and these allusions, in retrospect, point to a perfect storm. He was unready for such a powerful tide of somber, bleak artistry. And G.P. Landow's words above come very close to describing his feelings.

4. Goerge P. Landow, "British and European Aesthetes, Decadents, and Symbolists in the Victorian Web," Victorian Web, last modified September 17, 2002, http://www.victorianweb.org/victorian/decadence/decadence.html. Dr. Landow is professor of English and Art History at Brown University.
5. *The Man Who Was Thursday* (New York: Dodd, Mead and Co., 1908), iii.
6. *The Man Who Was Thursday*, iii.

It was Chesterton who felt overwhelmed by "a sense of loss, exile, isolation." Decades later, writing in his autobiography, he could still remember it all: "the whole mood, he wrote, "was overpowered and oppressed."[7]

But amid this troubled time, Chesterton found a salutary connection, though one unexpected, between Stevenson and Francis of Assisi.

It came from the realm of moral imagination. "The standpoint of romance," Chesterton disclosed, "is the soul of 'Treasure Island.'" Stevenson had a love

> for inanimate objects such as has not been known since St. Francis called the sun brother and the well sister. We feel that he was actually in love with the wooden crutch [Long John] Silver sent hurtling in the sunlight, [and] with the box that Billy Bones left at the "Admiral Benbow."[8]

It was a subtle thing, perhaps. But Stevenson's writings were life affirming. Writers can imbue the prosaic with things more deeply meaningful than we realize.

Chesterton saw this, and it was especially important to him, as Stevenson's artistic perspective stood in sharp contrast to the pervasive pessimism of literature and art in the 1890s. With a closer look at the passage

7. *Autobiography*, 92–93.

8. *Twelve Types* (London: Arthur L. Humphreys, 1902), 112–13.

already cited from his autobiography, we can get a still better sense of why Chesterton was drawn to Stevenson's moral imagination and considered it such a gift.

> This way of looking at things with a sort of mystical minimum of gratitude, was of course, to some extent assisted by those few of the fashionable writers who were not pessimists; especially by Walt Whitman, by Browning and by Stevenson; Browning's "God must be glad one loves his world so much", or Stevenson's "belief in the ultimate decency of things". But I do not think it is too much to say that I took it in a way of my own; even if it was a way I could not see clearly or make very clear. What I meant, whether or no I managed to say it, was this; that no man knows how much he is an optimist, even when he calls himself a pessimist, because he has not really measured the depths of his debt to whatever created him and enabled him to call himself anything. At the back of our brains . . . there was a forgotten blaze or burst of astonishment at our own existence. The object of the artistic and spiritual life was to dig for this submerged sunrise of wonder; so that a man sitting in a chair might suddenly understand that he was actually alive, and be happy.[9]

9. *Autobiography,* 94–95.

Chesterton's discovery of a "mystical minimum" brought life and sanity—even joy. As the novelist Frederick Buechner has said memorably, Chesterton "was filled with both an enormous sense of thankfulness, and an enormous need for someone or something to thank."[10]

So it was that a notebook Chesterton started in the autumn of 1894 was a wholly different repository of his thoughts from earlier journals that had been filled with morbid things.[11] His biographer Maisie Ward later described this new spirit. "Each day," she said, "seemed a special gift; *something that might not have been.*"[12]

Much of this good was owing to the stubborn, piercing light that shone on many a page of Stevenson's books. Chesterton gratefully acknowledged this, saying: "[Stevenson's] novels were only the two or three of his soul's adventures that he happened to tell. But he died with a thousand stories in his heart."[13]

Here, Chesterton might wish to say one thing more as this tavern visit ends. Stevenson's family, he knew, had for many years built lighthouses by the sea.

Stevenson's writings were like that: a beacon in time of storm. Or to use another image Chesterton had

10. Frederick Buechner, *Speak What We Feel* (New York: HarperCollins, 2001), 119.

11. William Oddie, *Chesterton and the Romance of Orthodoxy* (New York: Oxford University Press, 2009), 156.

12. Ward, *Gilbert Keith Chesterton*, 62. Emphasis added.

13. *Twelve Types*, 119.

written himself: "against the black flag of pessimism, [Stevenson's] flag really was a Moral Emblem."[14]

Chesterton rallied to that banner.

And one of the last things he ever said of Stevenson was among the best—speaking of their family tradition, the design of lighthouses, and how, in a very real sense, Stevenson carried that old and vital tradition into the world of literature. It cast the best metaphor Chesterton knew to describe a great debt:

> Stevenson . . . was the son of a house of highly respected architects of lighthouses; and nothing could be more really romantic than such a legend of men, *laboriously lifting the star-crowned towers of the sea.*[15]

14. G.K. Chesterton, *Robert Louis Stevenson* (New York: Dodd, Mead & Co., 1928), 81.

15. *Robert Louis Stevenson*, 6.

CHAPTER SEVEN

The Sage of Simple Gifts

We may not with the widest lives enlarge His liberty,
Whose wings are wider than the world.

—FROM "A SONG OF GIFTS TO GOD" (1913)

As a writer, Chesterton had a vast literary output. He published, according to one scholarly estimate, some seventy-eight books in all.[1] But of these, he wrote relatively few books about one person alone. One was devoted to Francis of Assisi, so for our seventh Fleet Street Tavern gathering, it would not

1. See M.F. McCauley's review of Alzina Stone Dale's Chesterton biography, *The Outline of Sanity,* in the September 1983 issue of *Commonweal* magazine, where it is stated, "Dale examines the Chestertonian corpus, seventy-eight books." The tally of seventy-eight books published by Chesterton was also confirmed in Stefan Kanfer's February 14, 1983, review of *The Outline of Sanity* for *Time* magazine, http://content.time.com/time/magazine/article/0,9171,953723,00.html.

be surprising to learn that Chesterton wished to talk about this medieval monk and saint. And he might well tell us, at the outset, that while he understood how fitting these titles were, he saw Francis in yet another way: with a poet's eyes.

Chesterton's lifelong interest in this medieval saint began in boyhood days, when his parents read to him "the story of Saint Francis."[2]

Then, too, during his days at the Slade School of Fine Art—or about the year 1894—Chesterton wrote about Francis to his friend Edmund Bentley.[3] Through many seasons of early life, this saint was a recurring figure.

This was certainly true in 1900. In December of that year, when Chesterton was twenty-six, he'd written about St. Francis in a review of James Adderley's book, *Francis: The Little Poor Man of Assisi*. Chesterton's lucid, influential review ran in the pages of the *Speaker* magazine.

All the same, a book review might not have seemed the most propitious place to express a debt of enduring gratitude, but James Adderley's book provided just that opportunity. It was the perfect "point of departure" for Chesterton to explore things St. Francis meant to him.

2. Alzina Stone Dale, *The Outline of Sanity: A Biography of G.K. Chesterton* (Grand Rapids: Eerdmans, 1982), 15.

3. Ward, *Gilbert Keith Chesterton*, 54.

To begin with, Chesterton said this saint was "one of the most extraordinary men that ever lived."[4] But not for reasons commonly thought of.

Some might connect the word *extraordinary* with "intellectual eminence." But that wasn't Chesterton's intent. Others might connect the word *extraordinary* with a great military figure. Yet, as he said, "a man might be as able as Julius Caesar and remain profoundly uninteresting."

No, there were other things to consider. So, as Chesterton wrote,

> Francis was extraordinary in this truer and higher sense, that he was one of those men who arise with an absolutely original vision of things inside their heads, who create the only indestructible thing—an atmosphere. With each of such men there is truly made a new heaven and a new earth, for they do not see the heaven and the earth that others see.

There were clues written in the world, and Chesterton's gratitude for them flowed from "the new way of seeing" that Francis set forth. In truth, it was really a very old way of seeing. But it was a way of seeing whereby Francis found the grace of memory. For Chesterton,

4. This and the remaining quotes in this chapter are from "St. Francis of Assisi," in the *Speaker*, December 1, 1900: 238–39.

one had only to contrast Francis with other great spiritual and philosophical leaders from the past to discern this. As he wrote,

> If Buddha, Plato and St. Francis had looked at the same tree they would have been standing in three different worlds. Buddha would have seen in the tree a gross embodiment in which a celestial force was immured, a spirit in a disgraceful incognito. Plato would have seen it as the shadow of a perfect tree existing in the ideal world. Francis would have seen it simply as "Brother Tree," an individual neighbour in the parish of the Cosmos, a silent but amusing companion, a man, as it were, with green hair and one leg.
>
> The whole conception was founded, of course, on the Christian doctrine of the great Father whose memory was an unending chronicle, in which the name of every stone or weed was clearly written. But he gave to the doctrine an individual turn of extraordinary beauty and humour by this notion of finding gossips and kinsfolk everywhere.

Here, Chesterton perceived a "blaze of benediction" in the things St. Francis taught: they came from "the place of poetry." His "literary instinct" was

> shown in his naming the fire "brother" and the water "sister," [and] the quaint demagogic dexterity of the

> appeal in the sermon to the fishes "that they alone were saved in the Flood." In the amazingly minute and graphic dramatisation of the life, disappointments and excuses of any shrub or beast that he happened to be addressing, his genius has a curious resemblance to that of [the Scottish poet Robert] Burns.

At the same time, Chesterton saw similarities in these "poems" of St. Francis, and "the more idealistic odes of [Edmund] Spenser." The conception of both, Chesterton said, "is sometimes almost indecipherable, for the poet draws in silver upon white." Further, in still other teachings of St. Francis, Chesterton discovered precious shards of paradox, and these of a very high order.

These shards were poems writ small; set with glorious contrast. Chesterton knew many might think this "a fascinating inconsistency," but he grew to love and cherish it. "Francis," he said,

> expressed in loftier and bolder language than any earthly thinker the conception that laughter is as divine as tears. He called his monks the mountebanks of God. He never forgot to take pleasure in a bird as it flashed past him, or a drop of water as it fell from his finger: he was, perhaps, the happiest of the sons of men.

And if St. Francis was "the happiest of the sons of men," it is jarring to read Chesterton's words, just one sentence later, on the "negation" present in his teachings. Yet this wasn't a moment of censure. Chesterton's thoughts about the "negation" present in the teachings of St. Francis were really a *cause célèbre.*

Here Chesterton posed a series of searching questions, then called the roll of answers to them. "This man," he said of Francis,

> undoubtedly founded his whole polity on the negation of what we think the most imperious necessities; in his three vows of poverty, chastity, and obedience, he denied to himself, and those he loved most, property, love, and liberty. Why was it that the most large-hearted and poetic spirits in that age found their most congenial atmosphere in these awful renunciations? Why did he who loved where all men were blind, seek to blind himself where all men loved? Why was he a monk, and not a troubadour? These questions are far too large to be answered fully here, but in any life of Francis they ought at least to have been asked; we have a suspicion that if they were answered we should suddenly find that much of the enigma of this sullen time of ours was answered also. It might be suggested that youth is the austere thing; that wherever there is hope there is renunciation . . . . It may be that under

> their sombre gowns, it was the monks that were the spendthrifts of happiness and we who are its misers.

Striking juxtapositions often colored Chesterton's writing, and one did in the next passage he wrote. There, he placed a line from Lewis Carroll beside the teachings of St. Francis, to show a kind of affinity in both writers. If ever a passage was a study in imaginative apologetics, or casting highly original reasons for hope, this passage was.

"The general attitude of St. Francis," Chesterton wrote,

> like that of his Master, embodied a kind of terrible common sense. The famous remark of the Caterpillar in Alice in Wonderland—*"Why not"* impresses us as his general motto. He could not see why he should not be on good terms with all things. The pomp of war and ambition, the great empire of the Middle Ages and all its fellows begin to look tawdry and top-heavy, under the rationality of that innocent stare. His questions were blasting and devastating, like the questions of a child. He would not have been afraid even of the nightmares of cosmogony, for he had no fear in him. To him the world was small, not because he had any views as to its size, but for the reason that gossiping ladies find it small, because so many relatives

> were to be found in it. If you had taken him to the loneliest star that the madness of an astronomer can conceive, he would have only beheld in it the features of a new friend.

One line from Chesterton's review of James Adderley's book seemed almost prophetic, as it recalled St. Francis's solicitude for one of the most beloved animals Kenneth Grahame would make world famous just a few years later in his classic book *The Wind in the Willows,* published in 1908. "Francis," Chesterton had written, "always assumed that everyone must be just as anxious about their common relative, the water-rat, as he was." Lewis Carroll, Kenneth Grahame—the life of St. Francis called in a world of wonders for Chesterton.

At the close of this gathering at Fleet Street Tavern, it's worth re-stating that twenty-two years after Chesterton's essay in the *Speaker* magazine, he returned to St. Francis in a book-length study—yet one more expression of gratitude.

Titled *St. Francis of Assisi,* the book followed a great soul of the past who'd profoundly shaped Chesterton's future. This study challenged "mere chronology" through a moving tribute to the saint who lived, and lived so vibrantly, hundreds of years before his time. "We should turn to St. Francis," Chesterton wrote, in the spirit of thanks for what he has done. He was above all things a great giver; and he cared chiefly for the best kind of giving which is called thanksgiving. If another great man wrote a grammar of assent, he may well be said to have written a grammar of acceptance; a grammar of gratitude. He understood down to its very depths the theory of thanks; and its depths are a bottomless abyss. He knew that the praise of God stands on its strongest ground when it stands on nothing. He knew that we can best measure the towering miracle of the mere fact of existence if we realise that but for some strange mercy we should not even exist.[5]

5. *St. Francis of Assisi* (New York: George H. Doran, 1924), 230–31.

CHAPTER EIGHT

The Sage of Lichfield

Go humbly . . . it has hailed and snowed . . .
With voices low and lanterns lit;
So very simple is the road,
That we may stray from it.

—FROM "THE WISE MEN" (1913)

At the start of our eighth tavern gathering, it might come as something of a surprise to find Chesterton has a keen interest in recounting an experience from April 1907, when he wrote in the *Illustrated London News* of a conversation he'd had "with an honest young atheist."[1]

It seems that as they talked, Chesterton's friend "was very much shocked at my disputing some of the

1. "The Error of Impartiality," in *All Things Considered* (London: Methuen, 1908), 211. Originally printed as a column in the *Illustrated London News*, April 20, 1907.

assumptions which were absolute sanctities to him." These included "the quite unproved proposition of the independence of matter, and the quite improbable proposition of its power to originate mind."[2]

At length, Chesterton's young friend resorted to one question, which he "delivered with an honourable heat of defiance and indignation."

"Well!" he asked Chesterton,

> "can you tell me any man of intellect, great in science or philosophy, who accepted the miraculous?" I said, "With pleasure. Descartes, Dr. Johnson, Newton, Faraday, Newman, Gladstone, Pasteur, Browning, Brunetière—as many more as you please." To which that quite admirable and idealistic young man made this astonishing reply—"Oh, but of course they *had* to say that; they were Christians." First he challenged me to find a black swan, and then he ruled out all my swans because they were black. The fact that all these great intellects had come to the Christian view was somehow or other a proof either that they were not great intellects, or that they had not really come to that view. The argument thus stood in a charmingly convenient form: "All men that count have come to my conclusion; . . . *if they come to your conclusion, they do not count.*"[3]

2. "The Error of Impartiality," 211.

3. "The Error of Impartiality," 212. Emphasis added.

In this exchange, Chesterton spoke of Samuel Johnson as a man of intellect who accepted the miraculous. But Johnson was far more than that. For Chesterton, he was a guide through life, and a cherished source of hard-won wisdom.

As "a man of letters," or writer in many genres, Johnson was also one of Chesterton's favorite authors. He saw the "gigantic realism in Johnson's kindness," and things that gave him "hold upon generations of living men."[4] True, Johnson could be famously direct, and sometimes impassioned—thus loud in conversation. But even that had its reasons.

"There is nothing elaborate about [Johnson's] ethics," Chesterton asserted.

> He wants to know whether a man, as a fact, is happy or unhappy, is lying or telling the truth. He may seem to be hammering at the brain through long nights of noise and thunder, *but he can walk into the heart without knocking.*[5]

James Boswell, Chesterton said, once complained to Johnson in private, explaining that "he did not mind asperities while there were alone, but did not

4. G.K. Chesterton, "The Real Dr. Johnson," in *On Lying in Bed and Other Essays*, 207.

5. "The Real Dr. Johnson," 207. Emphasis added.

like to be torn to pieces in company." He then added an idle figure of speech, some trivial simile, to which Johnson replied, "Sir, that is one of the happiest similes I have ever heard."

Of this incident, Chesterton said: "There is no better test of man's ultimate chivalry and integrity than how he behaves when he is wrong; and Johnson behaved very well . . . . Finding that he had given pain, he went out of his way to give pleasure."[6]

And Chesterton saw that Johnson had hidden depths. In youth, Chesterton weathered storms of doubt and despair. Johnson had also known such times. When Chesterton spoke about them, admiration for Johnson's fortitude came through. "Standing by itself in the wilderness," Johnson's soul, he said, "was reverent, reasonable, rather sad and extremely brave."[7] In the same way, Chesterton's words about Johnson's final hours were deeply eloquent and moving:

> I will not say that he died alone with God, for each of us will do that; but he did in a doubtful and changing world, what in securer civilizations the saints have done. He detached himself from time as in an ecstasy

6. "The Real Dr. Johnson," 206–207.

7. "Dr. Johnson," in *G.K.C. as M.C.: A Collection of 37 Rare G.K. Chesterton Essays*, ed. J.P. Fonseka (Eugene, OR: Wipf & Stock, 2016), 66. This essay was originally published as the introduction to *Samuel Johnson*, ed. Alice Meynell (London: Herbert & Daniel, 1911).

> of impartiality; and saw the ages with an equal eye. He was not merely alone with God; he even shared the loneliness of God, which is love.[8]

Those who wrestle with somber times, and depression, need to know there are others who've walked the hard path they sometimes know. Johnson was a fellow pilgrim through the "sloughs of despond" Chesterton sometimes knew, and was most welcome as a friend from an earlier age.

Chesterton saw two essential elements in Johnson as a friend from the past. He put it this way: in classic texts like *The Vanity of Human Wishes* and *The History of Rasselas,* "we overhear Johnson in soliloquy," whereas James Boswell, as a biographer, discerned moments of comedy in Johnson "by describing his clash with other characters."[9]

His tavern talk among friends, Chesterton said, had "rollicking sagacity." Johnson's spirited repartee, sudden volleys of wisdom, or sallies to bring laughter, made his conversation sparkle like a "rattling kaleidoscope."[10]

Still, it was sometimes true, Chesterton admitted, that

> towards the end of an argument Johnson would shout rude remarks; but so have a vast number of the men,

8. "Dr. Johnson," 75.
9. "Dr. Johnson," 66.
10. "Dr. Johnson," 71.

> wise and foolish, who have argued with each other in taverns. The only difference is that Johnson could think of rather memorable remarks to shout. I fancy his friends sometimes blamed him, not because he talked for victory, but because he got it. [Yet] if the idea is that his eye was first on victory and not on truth, I know no man in human history of whom this would be more untrue. Nothing is more notable in page after page of Boswell's biography than the honest effort of Johnson to get his enormous, perhaps elephantine, brain to work on any problem however small that is presented to it, and to produce a sane and reliable reply. On the maddest stretch of metaphysics or the most trivial trouble of clothes or money, he always begins graciously and even impartially. The mountain is in travail to bring forth the mouse—so long as it is a live mouse.[11]

A vital part of Johnson's life, Chesterton saw, was "the history of those great friendships" with Boswell, with Edmund Burke, with Sir Joshua Reynolds, and the Thrales, "which fill the most inexhaustible of human books; those companionships which Boswell was justified in calling the nights and feasts of the gods." They gave a "thousand lights of laughter [and] encouragement."[12] That is no mean thing.

11. "Dr. Johnson," 68.
12. "Dr. Johnson," 65, 70.

Such times gave something more; they mark a word too seldom used now, *camaraderie*, or the trusted company of friends. Johnson's life bore testimony that we do well to find and treasure it. Camaraderie is a gift.

To be sure, Chesterton would have cherished Johnson's good company on one of the long nights Johnson so often spent at the Mitre tavern. But since that could never be, he was especially grateful for the fellowship of words Johnson left in his many books, and books about him.[13] This was just one reason why he said, with solemn mirth, "It is possible that there are still people in England who do not adore Dr. Johnson. These persons must be removed, if possible by persuasion."[14]

Johnson was also a man of many eccentricities—and, since Chesterton walked London's Fleet Street in a hat, cape, and sword-stick cane (hoping to be set upon by brigands, so he could *unsheathe* that sword-stick), he'd really no room to talk: he could appreciate what it was like to be colorful.

Still, one of Johnson's eccentricities was both enigmatic and touching.

Boswell tells us that Johnson frequently placed his hand on wood, as though prompted by some sense of sovereign hope, or perhaps to make a wish.

13. "The fellowship of words"—a phrase coined by the author (KB).

14. "The Real Dr. Johnson," 204.

No one really knew why Johnson did this. But Chesterton thought he did. Perhaps, this seemingly odd habit was a yearning for something more. Chesterton could understand that, and so the poet in him observed that

> whatever jest or sentiment or fancy first set Samuel Johnson touching the wooden posts, he never touched wood with any of the feeling with which he stretched out his hands to the timber of that terrible tree, which was the death of God, and the life of man.[15]

Reading these things, we begin to understand Chesterton's debt to Johnson— a man richly human, deeply devout, and a sage well met from the past.

And Chesterton knew how to pay his debts.

In 1903, praising *The Life of Samuel Johnson,* he said, "Boswell succeeded in giving a most intimate and powerful picture of a human being [and he] simply towers above the whole eighteenth century, as the one man who discovered . . . that in biography the suppression of a man's faults did not merely wreck truth, but wrecked his virtues. 'I will not,' he said, 'make my tiger a cat to please anybody.' Boswell's life is absolutely soaked with the weaknesses and vanities described with the clearness of an inspired affection."[16]

15. *The Everlasting Man* (New York: Dodd, Mead & Co., 1925), 117–18.

16. "Boswell," in *G.K.C. as M.C.*, 6–7. Originally published in the November 1903 issue of *Good Words.*

Then came a parting line of grace and insight.

It was true, Chesterton observed, that Boswell "paints [Johnson] in the street, but he sees his soul walking there in the sunlight."[17]

17. "Boswell," 5.

CHAPTER NINE

The Sage of Mythic Tales

O light uplifted from all mortal knowing,
Send back a little of that glimpse of thee,
That of its glory I may kindle glowing One tiny spark for all men yet to be.

—FROM "FRAGMENT FROM DANTE" (C. 1905)

As stated earlier, Chesterton was a famous journalist, and for many years he wrote for the *Daily News* of London. For one column, published in 1901, he noted that "one by one, the eminent novelists of the Victorian era are being born again to the democracy in the form of cheap editions."[1] It was yet another call to the past.

This might well prove a point of departure for talk during the ninth of our Fleet Street Tavern

1. This and the following seven quotes are from "George MacDonald and His Work," originally published in the *Daily News*, June 11, 1901. Emphasis added.

gatherings—for this observation led, in that same column, to a discussion of the Scottish writer George MacDonald—a cause for celebration in Chesterton's eyes, as he thought MacDonald

> one of the most remarkable men of our time. [And he] will be discovered some day, as Blake, another man of genius, artistically faulty, has been discovered: until then he will be, like Blake, neglected, contemned, and quarried industriously by people who wish to borrow ideas. If to be a great man is to hold the universe in one's head or heart, Dr. MacDonald is great. No man has carried about with him so naturally heroic an atmosphere.

These are lines of fulsome praise; but just *what,* to be precise, did Chesterton mean by it all? Slowly, in the text of his column, Chesterton scattered clues, thrown about with the purposeful abandon of one gladly acknowledging a mentor.

There was no mistaking the fact that Chesterton saw MacDonald this way.

He hardly ever used titles to refer to people he wrote about, yet throughout this long column, MacDonald was always "Dr. MacDonald." It was an unambiguous measure of great respect. "[He] seemed an elemental figure," Chesterton said, "a man unconnected with any particular age, a character in one of his own fairy tales, a true mystic to whom the supernatural was natural."

Strange to say, though, these words were from a review of a book Chesterton thought full of flaws. That book was *The Marquis of Lossie,* and Chesterton was blunt enough about its shortcomings. "It is not one of [MacDonald's] best," he wrote. "Artistically speaking, it teems with faults."

But, Chesterton said, it was precisely here that a great distinction was to be made. MacDonald's novel was deficient, but Chesterton's eye was drawn to it for other reasons. As he explained,

> almost all the faults of this novel *are the virtues of a fairy tale.* The clearness of the ethical issue, the unclouded war of light against darkness, with no twilight or scepticism or timidity; the elemental sense of landscape and of man as the child of Nature, the stainless heroism of the heroes, the patent deformity of the evil characters; all this shows a spirit which looks out upon the world with the young and innocent and terrible eyes of Jack the Giant-Killer. Dr. MacDonald is far too good a poet to be a good novelist in the highest sense; for it is the glory of the novelist to look at humanity from a hundred standpoints: it is the glory of the poet to look at it from one. Dr. MacDonald sees the world bathed in one awful crimson

> of the divine love; he cannot look through the green spectacles of the cynic.

This passage is a list of unexpected things, and fascinating by way of contrast. Yet these thoughts were really lines meant to set the stage: a prologue, as it were. Chesterton eloquently established MacDonald's claim to have written a fairy tale in the pages of *The Marquis of Lossie.* That was telling, and necessary. But the heart of Chesterton's review rested in sentences to follow.

"The interesting point about 'The Marquis of Lossie' is this," he said,

> and it contains the whole secret of Dr. MacDonald's work: It is the story of a young Scotch fisherman who, in his impregnable simplicity and honour, goes up to a fashionable house in London, in order to rescue a fashionable lady (whom he knows to be his half-sister) from a disgraceful *mariage de convenance.* The story, as I have said, is not told with anything like the full measure of Dr. MacDonald's art; it is difficult to lay one's finger on a single scene which is quite properly proportioned, which has not too much philosophy, and too little psychology. Yet the whole story is as vivid and as tense as a detective story. We read it with a profound sense of something,

> [though] we cannot tell what it is. Then it will all become clear to us if we happen to remember Dr. MacDonald's magnificent fairy tale, "The Princess and Curdie," [the story] of a miner-boy, who, under the mysterious commands of a fairy grandmother, goes to save a king and a princess from the plots of a monstrous and evil city. Suddenly we realize that the two stories are the same, that one runs inside the other, and that the realistic novel is the shell and the fairy tale the kernel. All the awkwardness, all the digression, all the abruptness or slowness of incident, merely mean that the hero longs to throw off the black hat and coat of Malcolm MacPhail, and declare himself as Curdie . . . . All the excitement of the story lay in the fact that we knew that he was so.

This was MacDonald's great secret, and the very thing Chesterton found most meaningful. Seeing MacDonald first as a writer of mythic tales, he could see why thematic conceits like a "conception of . . . vigilance," and "universal power" permeated MacDonald's best writings, lending "the unfathomable gravity of complete happiness, the gravity of a child at play." In a word, these writings held mystical light from the realm of faith—and that light was, as J.R.R. Tolkien would say, refracted to many hues. Chesterton described it this way:

> A curious glow pervades [Dr. MacDonald's] books: the flowers seem like coloured flames broken loose from the flaming heart of the world: every bush of gorse is a burning bush, burning for the same cause as that of Moses. This sense of a perfect secret almost painfully kept by the universe is what shames the weariness of modern mystics. As if anyone who knew a secret could be weary.

Place this passage alongside lines from Tolkien's poem "Mythopoeia," and the similarities of artistic worldview are at once clear. Chesterton's reflections confirm these telling similarities, though of course he wrote about them long before Tolkien wrote his poem, or became famous. Here are lines from "Mythopoeia":

> The heart of man is not compound of lies,
> But draws some wisdom from the only Wise,
> And still recalls Him . . .
> Man, Sub-creator, the refracted light
> Through whom is splintered from a single White
> To many hues, and endlessly combined
> In living shapes that move from mind to mind.[2]

Mythic worlds that betoken the realm of faith—each a reason why Chesterton was forever indebted to

2. J.R.R. Tolkien, "Mythopoeia," quoted in Humphrey Carpenter, *J.R.R. Tolkien: A Biography* (New York: Houghton Mifflin, 2000), 194.

George MacDonald, a sage of generations past. In this first important column from Chesterton on MacDonald's art, much was revealed. And more would follow four years later, in a second piece.

* * *

This second column, called "The Sage," appeared in 1905. It was a long, well-considered tribute to MacDonald, who had recently passed away. Almost the first sentence gave this startling phrase: "If we test the matter by strict originality of outlook, George MacDonald was one of the three or four greatest men of 19th century Britain."[3]

To explain what he meant, Chesterton said, there was a "peculiar quality" to be noticed in the works of "almost every man with a novel point of view."

Next, Chesterton said something not at all complimentary: MacDonald had "a tendency to become for a time unaccountably weak and obvious, to labour the simplest pieces of sentiment, to write pages of platitude."

But, Chesterton stated, this very trait "exists par excellence in the original men. It was so with Dickens. It was so with Victor Hugo. It was so with Ruskin. It

3. This and the remaining quotes in this chapter are from "The Sage," *Daily News,* September 23, 1905. Emphasis added.

was so with Thackeray. It was most assuredly so with George MacDonald."

However, as Chesterton went on to suggest,

> those bursts of mysterious dullness or mysterious feebleness are, as . . . suggested, the direct product of the writer's bold independence and intense originality. He is so independent of conventions that he becomes conventional by accident. He is so unconscious of the beaten track that he even walks in it.

This was all fair enough, but how did one properly fathom a singular writer like MacDonald? To do this, Chesterton felt it was

> necessary to remember a type of man who is a pillar of simple societies, but whom complex societies tend to turn into something else. I mean the sage, the sayer of things. He is not the poet, for he does not sing; he is not the prose writer, for generally he cannot write. The things he produces form an artistic class by themselves; *they are logia or great passionate maxims, the proverbs of philosophy.*

The American Walt Whitman, in Chesterton's view, was such a writer. "Critics," Chesterton observed, "fuss themselves for ever about whether he was a poet or a prose writer. As a matter of fact, he was neither a poet nor a prose writer; he was a sayer of great things." And one of these great things was "a sort of primeval epigram," such as: "I do not give lectures, or a little charity; when I give, I give myself."

Likewise MacDonald, Chesterton said, "was in the same way not a born writer; he was a born maker of spontaneous texts." And also, "just as Whitman had to label his tracts of truth 'poetry,' MacDonald labelled his 'novels.'"

Building on this, Chesterton said MacDonald "was not so much a man of letters, then, as a man with something to say." However, the very thing he had to say was "something not easily understood."

That something was "the secret of the Cosmos"—a secret because it seemed *"too good to tell."* Here, Chesterton said, "The stars and all things" in MacDonald's world resonated with a perceptible kind of tension: for he believed "the pity of God was so positive as to be a definite passion like thirst; it was a fierce tenderness."

A mystic like MacDonald, Chesterton explained, "believes that a rose is red with a fixed and sacred redness, and that a cucumber is green by a thundering decree of Heaven. Hence in all the great Christian Mystics, in St. Francis, in [Thomas] Vaughan, in MacDonald, there is a brightness of colour."

In a word, MacDonald knew divine artistry had shaped the world.

He shared what he knew in his books. He was a sage from the past; teaching Chesterton many things good, and right, and true.

* * *

Chesterton's last words for MacDonald recall a benediction: an expression of profound gratitude that this Scottish writer had shared all he could about the secret of the cosmos. Chesterton listened—and believed. He closed with these thoughts: "actuality is the keynote of Mysticism." MacDonald was "a great man," and one now gone deeper into a world of actuality, and deepening joy.

CHAPTER TEN

The Sage of Celestial Things

To an open house in the evening
Home shall men come,
To an older place than Eden
And a taller town than Rome.

—FROM "THE HOUSE OF CHRISTMAS" (C. 1911)

To start the tenth and last of our Fleet Street Tavern gatherings, a question is put to Chesterton: "What is one of the more unlikely sources of wisdom you've met with in your travels?"

One answer he might give is the name John Bunyan.

One might think that, as a cultured man of Edwardian England, Chesterton had little to learn from a metalsmith born in the 1600s, with a modest education. Yet John Bunyan gave Chesterton timeless things; all through the powerful masterwork he began writing while wrongly imprisoned: *The Pilgrim's Progress.*

It is astonishing to learn just how often Chesterton wrote about Bunyan, and to what length. Bunyan figured prominently in several essays, and Chesterton wrote two specially commissioned pieces for books by, or related to, Bunyan. One was an introduction for *The Pilgrim's Progress,* published in 1904—the other a preface for the book *Christiana and Her Children,* published in 1914.

These writings were important, and more will be said about them below. But perhaps the most revealing thing Chesterton ever wrote about Bunyan came in a discussion of Bunyan and Shakespeare, in lines Chesterton wrote about his famous friend George Bernard Shaw. "A legend," Chesterton wrote,

> has run round the newspapers [saying] Bernard Shaw offered himself as a better writer than Shakespeare. This is false and quite unjust; Bernard Shaw never said anything of the kind. The writer whom he did say was better than Shakespeare was not himself, but Bunyan. And he justified it by attributing to Bunyan a virile acceptance of life as a high and harsh adventure, while in Shakespeare he saw nothing but profligate pessimism, the *vanitas vanitatum* of a disappointed voluptuary. According to this view Shakespeare was always saying, "Out, out, brief candle," because his was only a ballroom candle; while

> Bunyan was seeking to light such a candle as by God's grace should never be put out.[1]

When Chesterton said this, Shaw was at the height of literary celebrity. And such fulsome praise of Bunyan genuinely enhanced Bunyan's literary reputation.[2] During recent years, it had suffered somewhat; thus Chesterton's reflections about Bunyan, vis-à-vis Shaw, could not have come at a better time.

But in truth, this was just the beginning of Chesterton's myriad expressions of debt to Bunyan, a writer who died nearly two hundred years before he was born.

* * *

What was Chesterton's view of Bunyan's place in literature?

In *A Short History of England,* he said forcefully, "One of the very greatest and most human geniuses of the not very human seventeenth century was John Bunyan. His work is rightly regarded as a model and monument of completed English."[3]

1. *George Bernard Shaw* (New York: John Lane, 1909), 101–102.
2. *The Cambridge Companion to Bunyan,* ed. Anne Dunan-Page (Cambridge: Cambridge University Press, 2010), 85. Here Chesterton is described as one of Bunyan's "distinguished apologists in the twentieth century."
3. "Introduction to a New Edition," in *A Short History of England* (London: Chatto & Windus, 1917), x.

Chesterton also ranked *The Pilgrim's Progress* alongside William Langland's classic alliterative poem, *Piers Plowman*. Both, Chesterton observed memorably, are "symbolical pageants of human life under the light of religion."[4]

In another setting, Chesterton likened Bunyan to Honoré de Balzac, saying,

> The Catholic type of Christian ethics runs through Balzac's books, exactly as the Puritan type of Christian ethics runs through Bunyan's books. What his professed opinions were I do not know, any more than I know Shakespeare's; but I know that both those great creators of a multitudinous world made it, as compared with other and later writers, on the same fundamental moral plan as the universe of Dante.[5]

This was rare and celebrated company. Clearly, as a literary critic, Chesterton wished to render good service to Bunyan—who'd taught him things worth keeping.

Still another prominent writer, Sir Arthur Bryant, thought Chesterton and Bunyan themselves were much alike. "Gilbert Keith Chesterton," Bryant wrote, "spent his whole life in teaching others how to live. The very sound of his name is like a trumpet-call . . . . He

4. *A Short History of England*, x.
5. *The Superstition of Divorce* (New York: John Lane, 1920), 41.

was the kind of man of whom Bunyan was thinking when he drew the picture of Mr. Greatheart. His sword was at the service of pilgrims."[6]

* * *

In 1904, as said above, Chesterton stated many facets of his appreciation for Bunyan. He did so with a fine introduction for Cassell's new edition of *The Pilgrim's Progress.*

Here, after giving the humble circumstances of Bunyan's birth, Chesterton said, "His family was a good example of a thing of which there are many examples, and of which there cannot be too many—a sort of . . . aristocracy, plain and insignificant in name and handicraft, but rooted in the land like a royal dukedom."[7]

Many scenes from Bunyan's life and time spoke powerfully to Chesterton. One was Bunyan's time as a soldier, another the "sudden isolation" forced upon him when he was "arrested for having preached to unlawful assemblies, and imprisoned in Bedford Gaol."[8]

6. Quoted in D.J. Conlon, ed., *G.K. Chesterton: The Critical Judgments 1900–1937,* (Antwerp: Antwerp Studies in Literature, 1976), 535. Bryant's tribute originally appeared in the October 31, 1936, edition of the *Illustrated London News,* 764.

7. From Chesterton's introduction to Bunyan's *The Pilgrim's Progress* (London: Cassell, 1904), 5.

8. Introduction to Bunyan's *The Pilgrim's Progress,* 6.

It was then, Chesterton said, Bunyan first began to write, and "opened the first window on the dark and amazing drama which had been going on within," during such times as he "leaned on his pike, by the watch fires of the great war."[9] Concerning *The Pilgrim's Progress* itself, Chesterton marshaled a fascinating set of images to underscore its timelessness. His thoughts were eloquent and moving.

"That the prose poem," he said,

> which is so much nobler than most poetical poems after the Elizabethan age, should be used to help our sailors is more suitable than it seems. Bunyan was a Midland man, if ever there was one; and there is not, I think, in his wonderful fairy tale so much as a whisper of the sea. Yet he was of the sort that might have been a sailor as he was a soldier; and there is in his book a sort of knarled goodness such as sailors know . . . .
>
> For Bunyan the Midlander was right. When we send forth our sailors, we do not fear the wide seas, but only the narrow river. Mere distances are not appalling; rather they are pleasing; productive of welcomes and of travellers' tales. The tenderness felt for sailors, by all that humanity that can be called human, is due to their daily proximity to that dark rivulet which Bunyan found flowing through

9. Ibid.

> Bedfordshire, and which flows through every land and sea. We love these men because they are always threatened; and we like any institution which may enable such threatened men to live long.[10]

Reading this, one recalls something Chesterton admired in *Robinson Crusoe*: the image of sailors who are threatened, yet find, amid the dangers of the sea, a haven where good things are kept and treasured. This elemental aspect was something Chesterton considered at length. As he saw it, Bunyan's masterwork

> certainly exhibits all the marks of such a revival of primitive power and mystery. Its resemblance to the Bible is not mere imitation of style; it is also a coincidence of mood. Bunyan, who was a soldier in Cromwell's army, had himself been thrown into a world almost as ferocious and obscure as that of Gideon, or the Maccabees . . . . Nowhere, perhaps, except in Homer, is there such a perfect description conveyed by the use of merely plain words. The description in Bunyan of how Moses came like a wind up the road, and was but a word and a blow; or how Apollyon straddled quite over the breadth of the way and swore by his infernal den—these are things which can only

10. Preface to Mrs. Duncan Pearce's adaptation of *Christiana and Her Children* (London: Longmans Green, 1914), 9.

> be paralleled in sudden and splendid phrases out of Homer or the Bible, such as the phrase about the monstrous and man-killing hands of Achilles, or the war-horse who laughs at the shaking of the spear.[11]

To discern Homeric elements in Bunyan was a new and deeply important contribution to writings on the place of *The Pilgrim's Progress* in English culture. Here Chesterton offered telling comparisons, amid moments of great praise.

* * *

Not least among the facets of Chesterton's debt to Bunyan, we may note the way Bunyan's autobiography, called *Grace Abounding*, spoke so profoundly to him.

"No one," Chesterton said,

> can ever forget the impression of that awful chapter in "Grace Abounding," in which the sinner takes refuge in place after place only to expect that roof after roof will crash down upon him, and that he is safe nowhere if the very Universe that he inherits belongs to one who is his enemy. Nor will anyone forget the chapter in which the sinner is reconciled to the Universe, and walks about the fields, and

11. Introduction to *The Pilgrim's Progress*, 11–12.

> cannot forbear from talking to the birds about the great mercy of God.[12]

These lines reveal Chesterton's debt to Bunyan, despite humble origins, education, and circumstances. Truth, beauty, and art *lived* in Bunyan's book.

What's more, timeless things always caught Chesterton's eye; and they graced *The Pilgrim's Progress.* He was also a traveler, and not a little of his understanding of pilgrimage flowed from myriad things Bunyan had written. He cherished Bunyan's "symbolic pageant of human life under the light of religion,"[13] and how beautifully it commended "the great mercy of God."[14] For this, our last Fleet Street Tavern gathering, Chesterton might well say there are few things better to take with us.

12. Introduction to *The Pilgrim's Progress,* 13.

13. *A Short History of England,* x.

14. Introduction to *The Pilgrim's Progress,* 13.

AFTERWORD

Retrospective & the Realm of Wisdom

The dignity of the artist lies in his duty of keeping awake the sense of wonder in the world.

—FROM THE *ILLUSTRATED LONDON NEWS* (1927)

As a student of art, and a gifted artist, Chesterton knew what it was to attend a retrospective exhibit of a painter's works.

Christianity held kindred promise for him: a *perpetual* exhibit—a retrospective of God's works, through ages past, that lent perspective and meaning to the future. Solace, beauty, wisdom—all these, and more, were in the halls of that great museum. It was a temple of timeless truth—a cathedral.

That is why Chesterton treasured sojourns in the past, *laudator acti temporis.*[1]

And to all those taken up solely with "the cult of the future," he could only offer a heartfelt plea: Why throw away "the good in the past" like so many artworks disdained, and no longer worth keeping?

In one of his books, called *The Defendant,* Chesterton offered reflections that cast this in sharp relief. He considered the word *progress*, and what modernity thought progress was. He spoke for the past.

Then, taking up his pen, he spoke of things many would consign to obscurity with scarcely a second thought. They deserved a better fate.

"Progress," he said,

> should be something else besides a continual parricide. [In these pages,] I have investigated the dust-heaps of humanity, and found a treasure in all of them. I have found that humanity is not incidentally engaged, but eternally and systematically engaged, in throwing gold into the gutter and diamonds into the sea. I have found that every man is disposed to call the green leaf of the tree a little less green than

1. "A praiser of the old and great." A translation of this Latin phrase given online by literary scholar M.D. Aeschliman, in "Christopher Ricks and the Saving Remnant," *National Review*, September 24, 2016: http://www.nationalreview.com/article/440366/bu-editorial-institute-dispute-ricks.

> it is, and the snow of Christmas a little less white than it is . . . .
>
> Therefore I have imagined that the main business of a man, however humble, is defence.[2]

Stewardship is the heart of what Chesterton meant. Gifts from the past are *entrusted* to us. To value them rightly, to discern them, and then pass them on—such is the call of the past. Chesterton heard that summons, and said yes. It had been an urgent anthem, speaking across the years.

And here, most truly, he would say "Amen" to these lines:

> Before the hills in honour stood,
> Or earth received her frame,
> From everlasting Thou art God,
> To endless years the same.
>
> Under the shadow of Thy throne
> Thy saints have dwelt secure—
> The realm of time is Thine alone,
> And Thou a Sovereign sure.
>
> Our God, our help in ages past,
> Our hope for years to come,

2. *The Defendant* (New York: Dodd, Mead & Co., 1902), 6.

Be Thou our guard, while life shall last,
And our eternal home.[3]

THE END

3. Adapted by the author from Isaac Watts, "Psalm XC. 1–5," in Isaac Watts, *The Psalms of David Imitated* (London: Clark, Ford, & Cruttenden, 1719), 229–30.

For Further Reading

Belmonte, Kevin. *Defiant Joy: The Remarkable Life and Impact of G.K. Chesterton*. Nashville: Thomas Nelson, 2011. A literary biography that explores Chesterton's life chronologically through his finest books, as each was published.

Belmonte, Kevin, ed. *The Quotable Chesterton: The Wit and Wisdom of G.K. Chesterton*. Nashville: Thomas Nelson, 2011. Modeled on Tyndale's classic text, *The Quotable C.S. Lewis,* this text presents nearly 900 passages, arranged alphabetically and traced to their original sources. Brief essays on each facet of Chesterton's literary life are interspersed throughout.

Chesterton, G.K. *Orthodoxy*. London: John Lane, 1908. Editions of this classic abound, but the Barnes & Noble Library of Essential Reading paperback (2007) is affordable and readily available. It has a fine introduction by Steven Schroeder, who wrote the introduction for Chesterton's book *Heretics*, also featured in the Barnes & Noble Library of Essential Reading (2007).

McGrath, Alister. *If I Had Lunch with C.S. Lewis*. Carol Stream, IL: Tyndale, 2014. One of the finest introductions to

Lewis's life and thought for a general audience. This book unfolds through a richly imagined series of meetings with Lewis. The exploration of Chesterton's influence on Lewis is a particular highlight.

Ward, Maisie. *Gilbert Keith Chesterton*. Oxford: Sheed & Ward, 2005. The author of this classic biography knew Chesterton personally, corresponded with surviving friends like George Bernard Shaw and H.G. Wells, and had access to many Chesterton papers lost during World War II. Now available in paperback, this long and richly detailed biography is a must-read.

Famous Praise for Chesterton

For a singular gift of paradox, for a deep reverence and a high wit, and most of all for a free and shamelessly beautiful English prose, he will never be forgotten.

—Orson Welles[1]

Chesterton's most notable talent was for the sudden crystallization of illuminating observations. It would be a good idea [for someone] to make a collection of these, like La Rochefoucauld's *Maximes*.

—Malcolm Muggeridge[2]

He was an artist as well as a writer and he sees life with an artist's eye. He wanted his readers to share

1. From Welles's Introduction to *Mercury Theatre on the Air's* staging of *The Man Who Was Thursday,* broadcast September 5, 1938.
2. Malcolm Muggeridge, *Things Past* (New York: William Morrow, 1979), 147.

that poetic vision, to see the romance and numinousness in commonplace things.

—P.D. James[3]

In some ways, [Chesterton's] books have become more a part of my mental make-up than those of any other writer you could name . . . I owe him a debt of gratitude of a kind which it is foolish to try and express in words.

—Dorothy L. Sayers[4]

At Wheaton [College] I am under the same roof with other authors I admire, like MacDonald, Tolkien, [and] Chesterton . . . "

—Madeleine L'Engle[5]

O Chesterton, but you are a darling! I have just read your "Dickens"— it's as good as Rabelais. Thanks!

—philosopher William James, author of *The Varieties of Religious Experience*[6]

3. P.D. James on GKC, quoted in *Father Brown: The Essential Tales,* (New York: The Modern Library, 2005), xiv-xv.
4. As quoted in Barbara Reynolds, "Dorothy L. Sayers and "The Surprise," in *The Chesterton Review,* August 1999, 307.
5. Alzina Stone Dale, "An Interview with Madeleine L'Engle," in *The Living Church* newsletter, (November 28, 1982), 9.
6. Quoted in Ian Ker, *G.K. Chesterton: A Biography* (Oxford: Oxford University Press, 2011), 184.

At Stowe, our English tutor was that remarkable falconer-pacifist-huntsman, T.H. White, who wrote *The Sword in the Stone* . . . . One morning Tim White came into our beautiful Georgian classroom and announced, "G.K. Chesterton died yesterday, P.G. Wodehouse is now the greatest living master of the English language."

—SIR IAIN MONCREIFFE[7]

The year I spent in England [after graduation from Harvard] I was very nervous and frightened, standing more or less on the threshold of my adult life and career, if any. One of the ways I assuaged my anxiety was to read a lot of Chesterton and C.S. Lewis.

—JOHN UPDIKE[8]

The case for Christianity in general is well given by Chesterton; and I tried to do something in my *Broadcast Talks.*

—C.S. LEWIS, ON THE INFLUENCE OF CHESTERTON AND THE RADIO TALKS LEADING TO *MERE CHRISTIANITY*[9]

7. Quoted in Joseph Pearce, *Wisdom and Innocence: A Life of G.K. Chesterton* (London: Hodder & Stoughton, 1996), 484.
8. Quoted in James Plath, *Conversations with John Updike* (Jackson: University Press of Mississippi, 1994), 187.
9. C.S. Lewis, quoted in P.F. Ford, ed., *Yours Jack: Spiritual Direction from C.S. Lewis* (New York: HarperOne, 2008), 155.

> [Chesterton's *Orthodoxy]* is a powerful intellectual defense of the rationality of the Christian faith, and especially its capacity to make sense of things. Christian doctrine is not something that was forcibly imposed upon reality, but rather the key that unlocks "life's real meaning." The Christian faith, he argued, was to be considered as a hypothesis which, once tested, can become a means of perception, making sense of what was previously obscure. While still an atheist, [C.S.] Lewis had been deeply impressed by Chesterton's *Everlasting Man;* his subsequent career could be seen as a gradual assumption of Chesterton's mantle as an apologist.
>
> —Dr. Alister McGrath, Oxford University[10]

> G.K. Chesterton once said that "the world would never starve for wonders, but only for the want of wonder."
>
> —Ronald Reagan[11]

One working title for this novel [*Brendan,]* was *A World of Crowns,* a phrase suggestive of Buechner's

10. Alister McGrath, *The Intellectual World of C.S. Lewis* (Chichester, England: Wiley-Blackwell, 2014), 9.
11. From President Ronald Reagan, "An Address to the Nation on Christmas," Thursday, February 24, 1981.

long-term preoccupation with laughter, or possibility, as the heart of things. He discovered the idea in Chesterton, and cites it as an epigram for *Brendan:* "In the very shape of things there is more than green growth; there is the finality of the flower. It is a world of crowns."

—W. Dale Brown, on G.K. Chesterton and the writing of Frederick Buechner's novel, *Brendan*[12]

During the 1908–9 school year, J.R.R. Tolkien presented two books by G.K. Chesterton to the King Edward's School library: Orthodoxy, published in 1908; and Heretics, published in 1905.

—from *The J.R.R. Tolkien Companion and Guide*[13]

Chesterton once said that it is our duty to keep the Flag of This World flying . . .

—J.R.R. Tolkien (1969)[14]

12. Brown, *The Book of Buechner* (Knox Press, 2006), 257; & Chesterton, *The Everlasting Man* (New York: Dodd, Mead, 1925), 331.
13. Christina Scull and W.G. Hammond, eds., *The J.R.R. Tolkien Companion and Guide* (Boston: Houghton Mifflin, 2006), 13.
14. Humphrey Carpenter, ed., *The Letters of J.R.R. Tolkien* (Boston: Houghton Mifflin, 1981), 402.7

Dear old G.K.C.—If after all my Atheology turns out wrong and your Theology right I feel I shall always be able to pass into Heaven (if I want to) as a friend of G.K.C.'s. Bless you.

—H.G. Wells (1933)[15]

I have not met G.K.C. [but] Shaw always calls him a man of colossal genius.

—T.E. Lawrence, "Lawrence of Arabia," on Chesterton and George Bernard Shaw (1932)[16]

15. Quoted in Maisie Ward, *Gilbert Keith Chesterton* (New York: Sheed & Ward, 1943), 604.

16. Quoted in *Gilbert Keith Chesterton*, 367.

Epigraph Sources

OPPOSITE TABLE OF CONTENTS

G.B. Shaw, "A Generous Opponent," in *The Mark Twain Quarterly,* (published by The International Mark Twain Society, 1936), page 9. The review Shaw refers to "The Position of Sir Walter Scott," published in the August 10, 1901, issue of *The Daily News*. While not mentioning *Ivanhoe* by name, the review does mention plot elements from the novel, such as "Athelstane's defiance of De Bracy," and words spoken by "Brian de Bois-Guilbert to Rebecca."

Garry Wills, *Chesterton* (New York: Doubleday, 2001), p. xvii.

Ernest Hemingway, "The Three-Day Blow," a short story from the book *In Our Time,* (Paris: Three Mountains Press, 1924).

PREFACE

William Oddie, *Chesterton and the Romance of Orthodoxy* (New York: Oxford University Press, 2009), 379.

CHAPTER ONE

G.K. Chesterton, *The Man Who Was Thursday and Related Pieces* (Oxford: Oxford University Press, 1996), 175.

CHAPTER TWO

G.K. Chesterton, "The Great Minimum," *Poems,* (New York: John Lane, 1915). These are lines from the poem, 48.

CHAPTER THREE

"The Ballade of a Book Reviewer," *Poems,* 151.

CHAPTER FOUR

"A Word," *Poems*, 80.

CHAPTER FIVE

"To Edmund Clerihew Bentley," *Poems*, 4–5. This poem was also used as the dedication in *The Man Who Was Thursday*.

CHAPTER SIX

Quoted in Maisie Ward, *Gilbert Keith Chesterton* (New York: Sheed & Ward, 1943), 62.

CHAPTER SEVEN

"A Song of Gifts to God,"*Poems*, 61.

CHAPTER EIGHT

"The Wise Men," *Poems*, 56.

CHAPTER NINE

"A Fragment from Dante," *Poems*, 68.

CHAPTER TEN

"The House of Christmas," *Poems*, 59.

AFTERWORD

Lawrence J. Clipper, ed., *The Collected Works of G.K. Chesterton, Vol. XXXIV: The Illustrated London News 1926–1928* (San Francisco: Ignatius Press, 1991), 313.

www.ingramcontent.com/pod-product-compliance
Lightning Source LLC
Chambersburg PA
CBHW021330060726
47591CB00006B/1954

* 9 7 8 1 9 5 4 8 8 7 2 0 6 *